Are You Hypnotized By The Dwarf Within

#96

Pamela Denise Brown

Author

Publisher

Illustrator

Editor

ACKNOWLEDGEMENT

I Would Like To Acknowledge The CREATOR OF HEAVEN AND EARTH (GOD) FOR ALL THAT HE HAS Given Me. Thanking God I Am For My Talents and Gifts.

I Recognize That The Lord Gave Me This Gift, Which Allows Me To Share With Children And Everyone That Participates In The Reading Of The Literary Material That I Produce Through The Commission Of God.

Thank You Lord God

I Will Forever Be Grateful

For Your Trust In Me

Pamela Denise Brown

Copyright © 2016 Pamela Denise Brown

All rights reserved. No part of this book may be used or reproduced by any means, graphic, electronic, or mechanical, including photocopying, recording, taping or by any information storage retrieval system without the written permission of the publisher except in the case of brief quotations embodied in critical articles and reviews.

Pamelainthelight Publications/Books Speak For You books may be ordered through booksellers or by contacting:

Books Speak For You
A Division Of Pamelainthelight Publications
Philadelphia, PA
Booksspeakforyou.com
Pamelainthelight.com
267-454-3317

The views expressed in this work are solely those of the author.
Any illustration provided by iStock and such images are being used for illustrative purposes.

Certain stock imagery © iStock.

ISBN:9781943611201
Library of Congress Control Number:

Printed in the United States Of America

Books Speak For You (Non Profit Children's Division)
A Division Of Pamelainthelight Publications

DEDICATION

I dedicate this book and EVERY BOOK I WRITE to my Mother (Queen-Ella Brown) who NEVER STOPS BELIEVING IN ME, WHO IS ALWAYS BY MY SIDE AND HAS ALWAYS PARTICIPATED IN THE SUCCESS OF WHO I AM AS A PERSON, THANK YOU MOM FOR BEING WHO YOU ARE.
To My children
Carrayah Queen-Ella,
Gabriel Joel
&
Carrynn Erin-Josette,
LOVING YOU THREE FOREVER I AM.
I also dedicate this book to all Children, Parents, Guardians, Mothers, Fathers, Teachers, Principals, Librarians, Pediatricians, Therapist, Counselors, Thought Leaders and every person that has anything to do with the positive and successful development of children in the world.
Continue to be an inspiration and motivator to the children that are entrusted to the cultivation of your expertise.

Thank You
I Remain,
Pamela Denise Brown

THE BOOKS

100 BOOKS IN 100 DAYS

I was commissioned by God to write 100 books in 100 days on October 1, 2015,

Completion Day January 8, 2016.

This is the **96TH** Book Of the 100.

My Collection Of Educational Books is designed to foster the social development of children. I believe the books I write will transform the minds of children. My Books are designed to effectuate change and influence success in the lives of children.

The Books in the Collection are Reinforcements to Learning. If understood and used in collaboration with the academic curriculum children are given, the books will help build their self-esteem and confidence to a level that would help them socially engage in a diverse world with confidence and ultimately prepare them for life.

Pamela Denise Browns' QUOTES

If You're In A "CROWDED" Room and A Child Is Sitting "ALONE" that can only mean the room is EMPTY.....

    11/21/2105 1:42 a.m.

Children Stand silently trying to open a door that cannot be opened with hands......

    11/23/2015 11:18 a.m.`

INTRODUCTION

Are You Hypnotized By The Dwarf Within IS A MUST READ......the book is educational and it talks about the draw that cell phones have on children in an uneducated alluring way. The story is told using 95 titles of the books that I've written in the 100 book collection. It takes a deep dark look into the hypnotism of a concentrate poetically, that is educationally dangerous to children. Are You Hypnotized By The Dwarf Within takes a serious look into what children are facing by not using the smart phone that was created to be used AS A S-M-A-R-T Phone…….

Every Book in the Collection is designed to effectuate change in the lives of children and influence success. In addition, the collection of books is tools to help children engage socially in a diverse world with confidence and ultimately prepare them for life. I believe the books in the Collection are also tools to psychologically rouse children to become positive, culturally sensitive, confident, unbiased and trustworthy and to have a sense of social consciousness to be socially aware.

Are You Hypnotized By The Dwarf Within

Are You Hypnotized By
The Dwarf Within —

Its duty is to leave you empty

And unattended —

Mesmerized under what seems to be the **help** —

A system that was put in place by someone that knows nothing about the disadvantage

You

Face.

And you still

get up..

Mesmerized by something

you know nothing

about —

The invasion ---

That has hypnotized you and caused you to look in a different direction.

Your focus has changed….

A disservice to the process of the development of your

mind,

Your person ---

Fighting to understand why you were sat in a corner –

NO

not literally –

hypothetically speaking,

You must be hypnotized by the dwarf within ---
-

A disservice to society –

by the people that sit in the dark room

With the door

Closed.....

The room is already dark …. And you have been invaded…..

The dwarf within,

YOU KNOW nothing about,

But yet you succumb to it,

Because you don't want to

FIGHT....

Maybe,

you don't know how....

To

FIGHT THAT IS...

The dwarf within your mind,

Captured by video games and

You're not trying to create a game yourself,

You have no interest in that.

You're just a player

of the game

In which you

play,

This is not the game

players play.

Players invent games

and

People who get played

Or

For lack of better words

people looking for

entertainment

Play them

With nothing else

IN MIND!!!!!

Your posture

Messed Up, why -

--

The dwarf within

You've been INVADED

and

You can't SEE,

Why

YOUR HEAD IS ALWAYS

HANGING

DOWN

D- O – W - N

That **SCREAM**

On the SCREEN ---

texting,

Day and night

And when you sleep,

You imagine

words

You want to say....

But this you do,

Does not include

Your

mouth,

Your

communication

TAKEN away ---

The dwarf within

or

Have you been

HYPNOTIZED

And no

You don't know how to

SPELL

Mesmerized by the dwarf

within ---

You have created your own language,

A set of words

That ONLY

MAKES SENSE TO

YOU

And

A small group of people

These people

DO NOT RUN

anything,

they don't run

the world,

they don't sit

in high places,

They don't achieve,

Why?

Their time is spent with

their

HEADS DOWN,

their faces on the screen

Don't you hear the

SCREAM ---

No,

because you've been

invaded by the dwarf

within ---

Mesmerized

or

Hypnotized

MESMERIZED

Or

HYPNOTIZED,

You are not who you could be,

Should be

And

Are

Capable

Of

Becoming.

A Disservice ...

And

This country you live in

--- LAND OF THE

FREE---

a

Disservice ---

You will grow up

And then

what?

An invasion ---

A million people like you,

speaking a language that only

A few understand

And a handful

know,

The dwarf within---

l-o-l, (laugh out loud)

w-y-d (what you doing)

Are you HYPNOTIZED? Either way,

you're

NOT

WINNING.

An invasion has occurred

and

You

CAN'T

SEE,

Why

Because you walk around with your HEAD

HANGING

DOWN

Always downward on that Screen —

LOOK UP

And think or maybe WONDER ---

Have you been HYPNOTIZED,

I know —

1. When I Think About Tomorrow

I WONDER

2. If Tomorrow Comes

WILL IT BE

3. Gone Too Soon

WILL I

4. Like School..

WAIT A MINUTE,

I'm not hypnotized,

but

5. I Thought I'd Dream

Of a better Today

So

6. Don't Turn Your Back

On Me

Because I am

worth saving.

Like the

7. Beauty In The Wind -

--

8. Here I Am –

Don't make

9. No Excuses

Just be there for me, wait a minute and watch what I do next

10. I Thought I'd Dance

For a better today.
I'm not Mesmerized,
I just need to

11. Think First

And no

12. It's Not Strength

It's my creator and

13. The Skies The Limit

So lets

14. Play Catch ---

And catch up, because

15. Moving Forward

Might Be Tight

SO

16. Don't Stop Now

17. You Can Do Anything

Be Anything

Become Anything

If you

can

18. See The Big Picture

So

19. Let's Stay Together While We Play Together And get the job done, I have

20. 50 Reasons Why

YOU, ME, WE

Should

21. Always Do The Right Thing

BECAUSE

22. Everything You Do Counts

EVERYTHINIG, FROM

23. Bike Rides

TO WALKS IN THE PARK

24. If You Get Up And Play

This game called LIFE with me, you'll see if you look close enough

25. I'm Happy With Me, My Mouth, My Eyes, My Face, My Ears, My Nose, My Height, I'm Happy With Me

And

You should be too.

26. If You Concentrate On The Right Things,

You'll understand and you'll see

27. Time Changes But The Rules Don't

So what's important is

28. Today We Learn

And we realize that

29. 4 Plus 4 Is Not 12

You shouldn't have to

30. Figure It Out

You should have understood a long time ago that there are lessons in life and

31. This Is All For You

So

32. When You Get Finished I Have Something Else For You To Do

All of this is to me and to

33. You First

All you have to do is be obedient and

34. Take Two Steps Not One

Because

35. You're Almost There

And please don't ask this question

36. Are You Finished Yet

Because

37. Time Goes By

So stop and

38. Share Your Story

Because

39. You Can Do This

If you

40. Add The Numbers Up

You'll realize

41. There Is No Competition We All Win

So keep your head up

and

42. Look Up

43. Who Am I

A child that wants you to realize that

44. I Want To Grow Up

And

45. Be Of Good Character

I know that

46. You're Not Too Young To Have Goals, Why, because

47. Mommy Taught Me That

And I realize that the cow did not jump over the moon

Or

Wait a minute,

48. Did The Cow Jump Over The Moon

I asked that question and I'll keep asking,

49. Should We Be Talking

Or should we pay attention?

50. It's Not Black Or White

And I

51. Believe In Happiness

So don't discount who I am

and

52. Don't Throw Trash Out The Window

53. We Are All In This World Together

And I know I like to

54. Ask Questions

Because, I'm what they

call

55. Psychologically Sociable

So

56. Did You Forget To Say Thank You?

Because

I just helped you out

And guess what,

I have a little secret,

57. I Know The Color Of The Sky

I'm excited about that,

I can't wait to share my story with everyone and actually read my story,

58. It's Good To Be Optimistic

You may see this as a

59. Journey Or Adventure

But I see you, shinning

60. There's A Star In Your Eye

And it's bright as you are,

always shining,

So you don't need to ask me,

61. Why Should I Try

We all should try,

I know

62. It's Good To Be Confident,

We also need to

63. Learn How To Be Grateful

Or at least read my 64th Book,

64. 6 Steps To change

And actually follow the steps.

Everybody knows

65. Recess Is Over

So hurry up and

66. Sit In Your Seat

And when you get up

67. Don't Get Out Of Line,

Because you will sure lose your place,

You don't understand what's going on

68. What Are You Going To Do If It's Too Late

So I ask you this day

69. What Motivates You

70. Are You Paying Attention

Or have you been mesmerized

Or hypnotized

By the dwarf

Within.

I can't understand

71. Why You Would Want to Get Out Of Line

All you have to do is

72. Manage Your Anger

And

73. Accept The Challenge

So if

or

74. When You Run Make Sure You're Not Running From Yourself

I really want to know

75. Who Are You Hiding From

Everybody knows that in this life,

76. One Day The Rules Will Matter

So

77. What Does A Name Mean

Or better yet

78. How Will They Describe You

What will they say?

Have you been

Hypnotized by the dwarf within

Holding your head down looking at the screen,

Don't you hear the **SCREAM** or are you………………..

Better yet

79. Don't Be A Dummy With A Smart Phone….

Don't limit yourself..

Don't let the dwarf within

win...

I don't know

Have you been hypnotized?

You have the wrong idea about this,

I want to help you,

But

80. The Differences Do They Really Matter

I really need to know,

Why you let your head

hang so **low**...

Looking at that screen.....

Do you

Know…

I want to know

81. What Color Is Your Blood

Is it the color of mine

You need to know

82. Disobedience Is Going To Cost you

We are all humans here

and

83. Everybody Deservers A Chance To Shine

Even you,

Lift your head...

Have you been hypnotized by the dwarf within...

You should already know the rules and

84. Thank You, Yes and Please The New Hello, Well ignorance Is Gone….. Yesterday forgotten

85. In The Morning I Rise and I understand

86. Discipline Is Good

And I also realize

87. The Law Is For The Lawless

So just take a Deep breath,

Lift up your head...

You're

Not

Hypnotized neither

Mesmerized

88. WOW Did I Do All That,

Wake up,

It's not a dream

89. Good Morning, I Hope Things Are Going Great Fantastic and Well For You

90. Now Swimming

That's Fun

But

91. What's A Flower

Something pretty I think

Look at how time has... flown by

92. You'll Be Saying I Remember When In A Minute

And

93. You're Going To Feel Good When It's all over

Question....

Just one Question...

94. Is Anger Your Friend

Or

Are you trying to do the right thing...

I know what I'm going to do.

95. I Decided To Take Door # 1 And not be mesmerized.....

96. Are You Hypnotized By The Dwarf Within...

GONE TOO SOON
Pamela Denise Brown

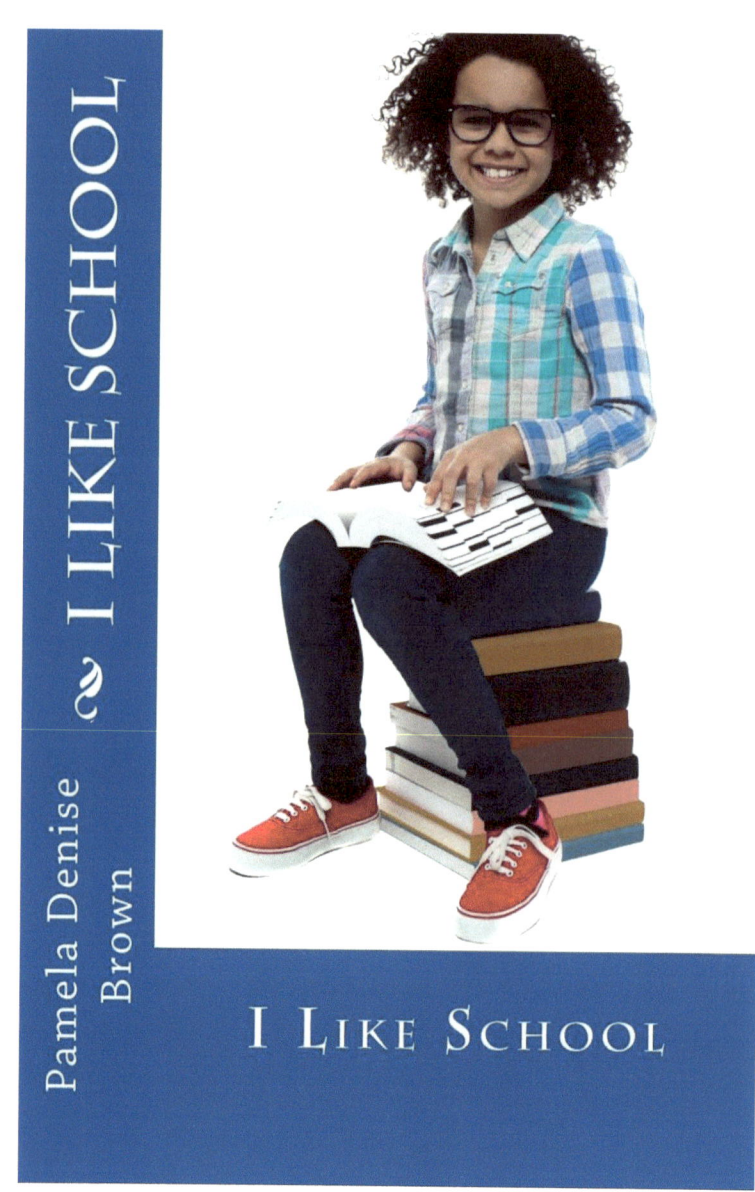

I THOUGHT I'D DREAM

Pamela Denise Brown

Wind is strong, it pushes you from side to side and then it puts you back in place,

The same wind that just stroked, caressed, embraced your face.......

BEAUTY IN THE WIND

PAMELA DENISE BROWN

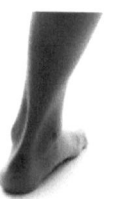

I THOUGHT I'D DANCE

Pamela Denise Brown

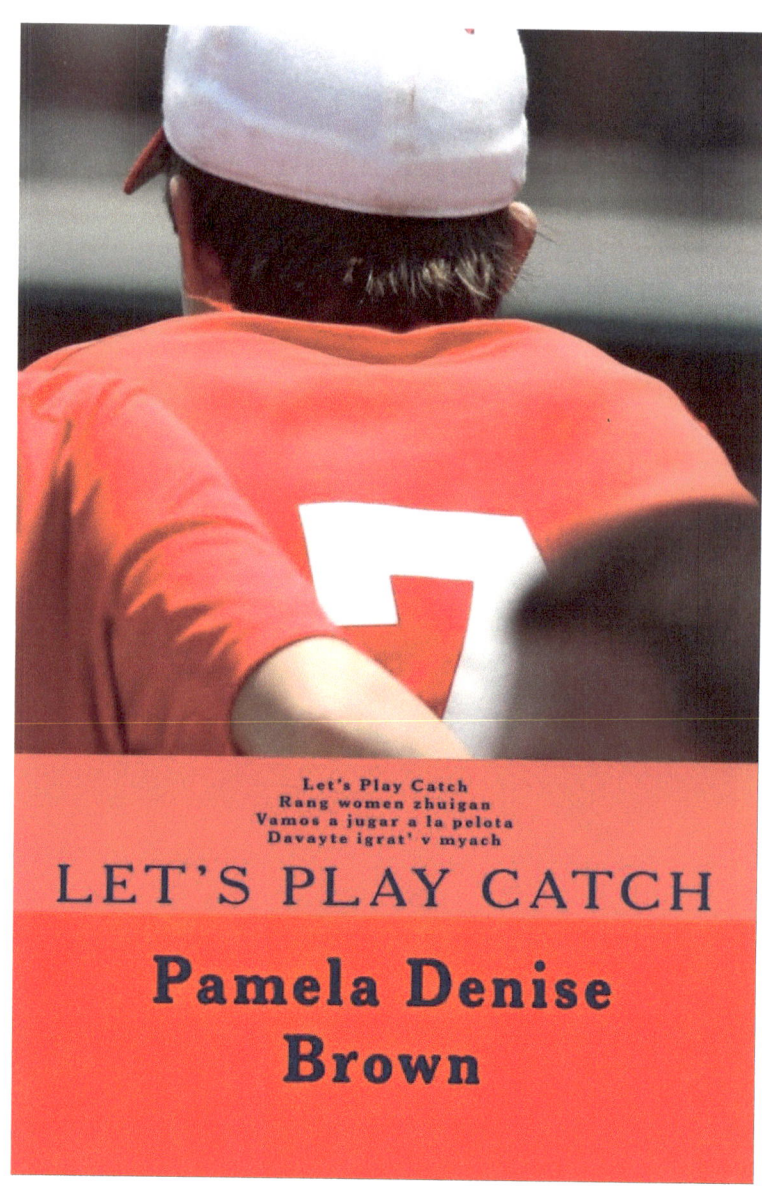

MOVING FORWARD MIGHT BE TIGHT

Pamela Denise Brown

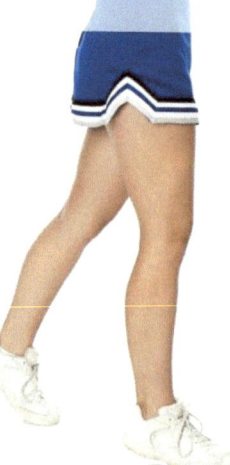

Don't Stop Now
KEEP MOVING FORWARD

Pamela Denise Brown

SEE THE BIG PICTURE

Voir la grande image

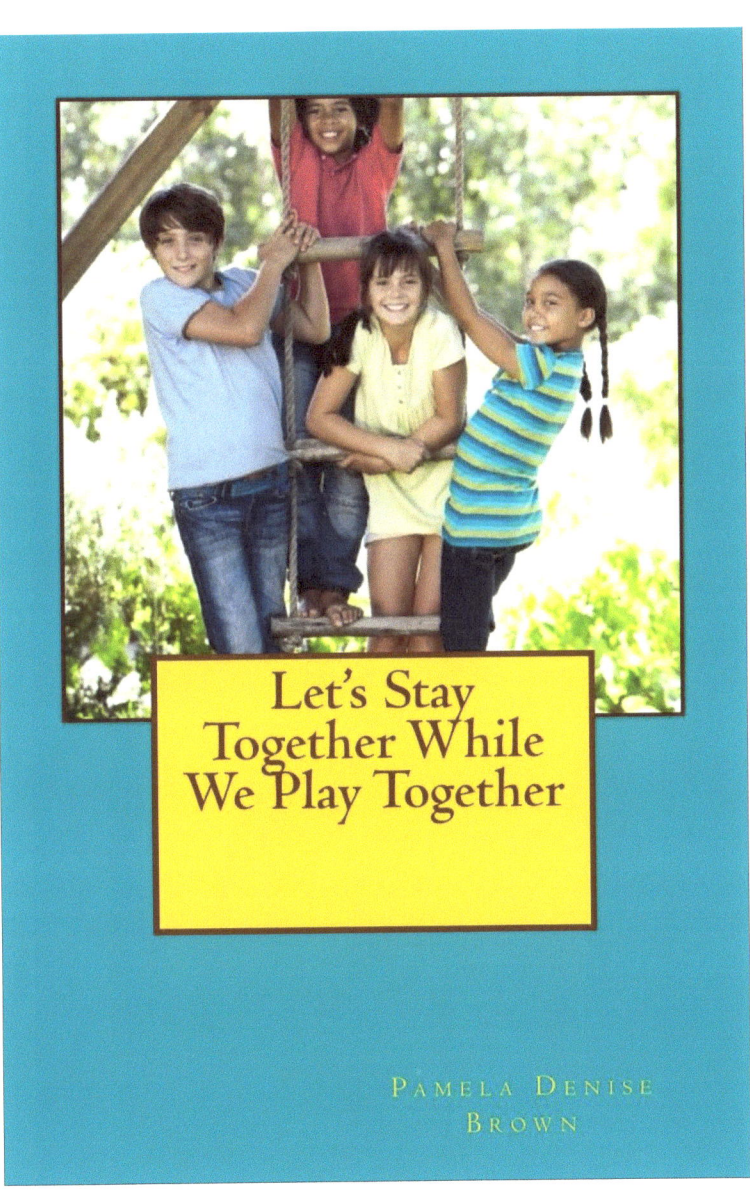

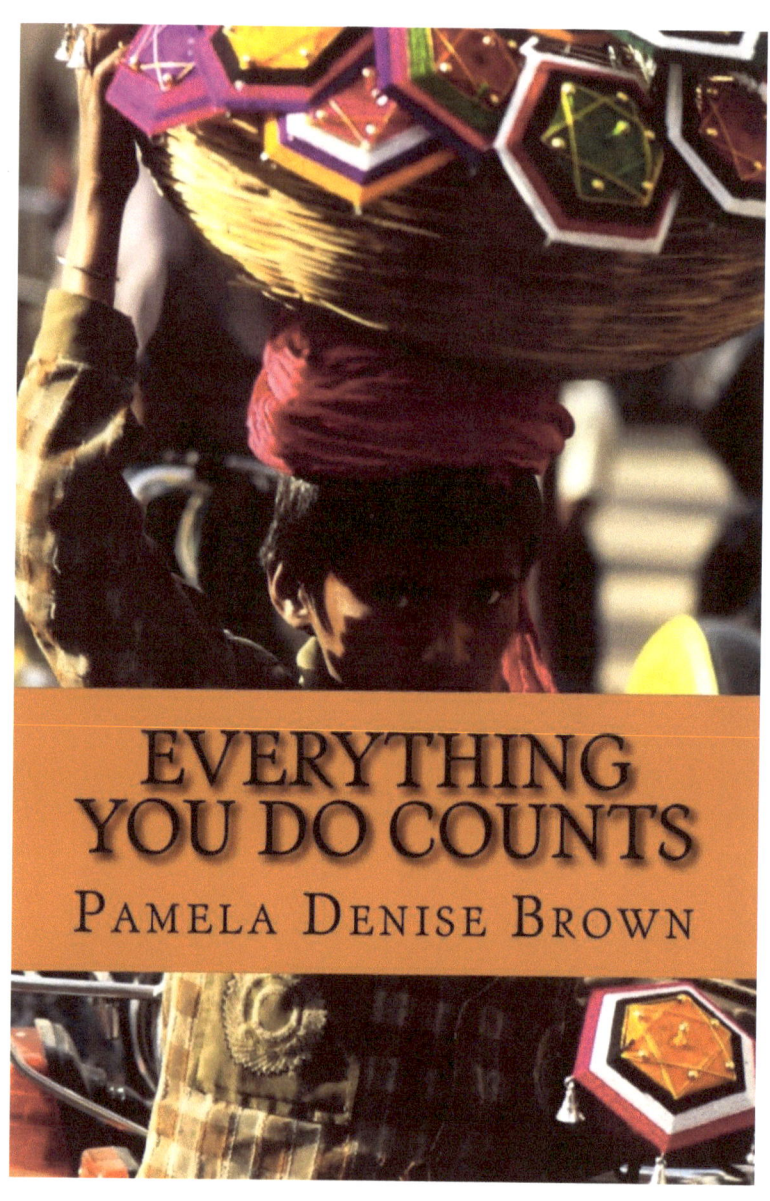

Get Up And Play
Dapatkan Up Dan Play
Pamela Denise Brown

I'm Happy With Me

My Skin, My Mouth, My Eyes, My Face, My Ears, My Nose, My Height

Pamela Denise Brown

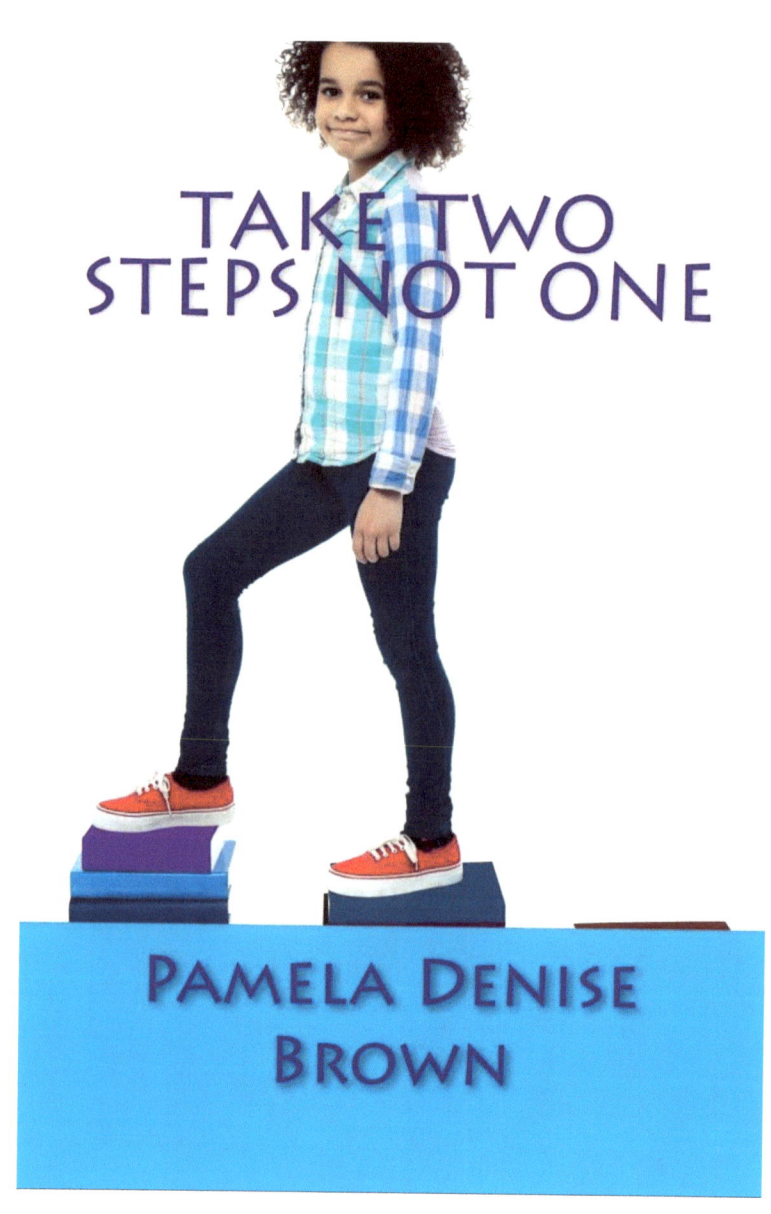

ADD THE NUMBERS UP

ANADIR LOS NUMEROS ARRIBA

PAMELA DENISE BROWN

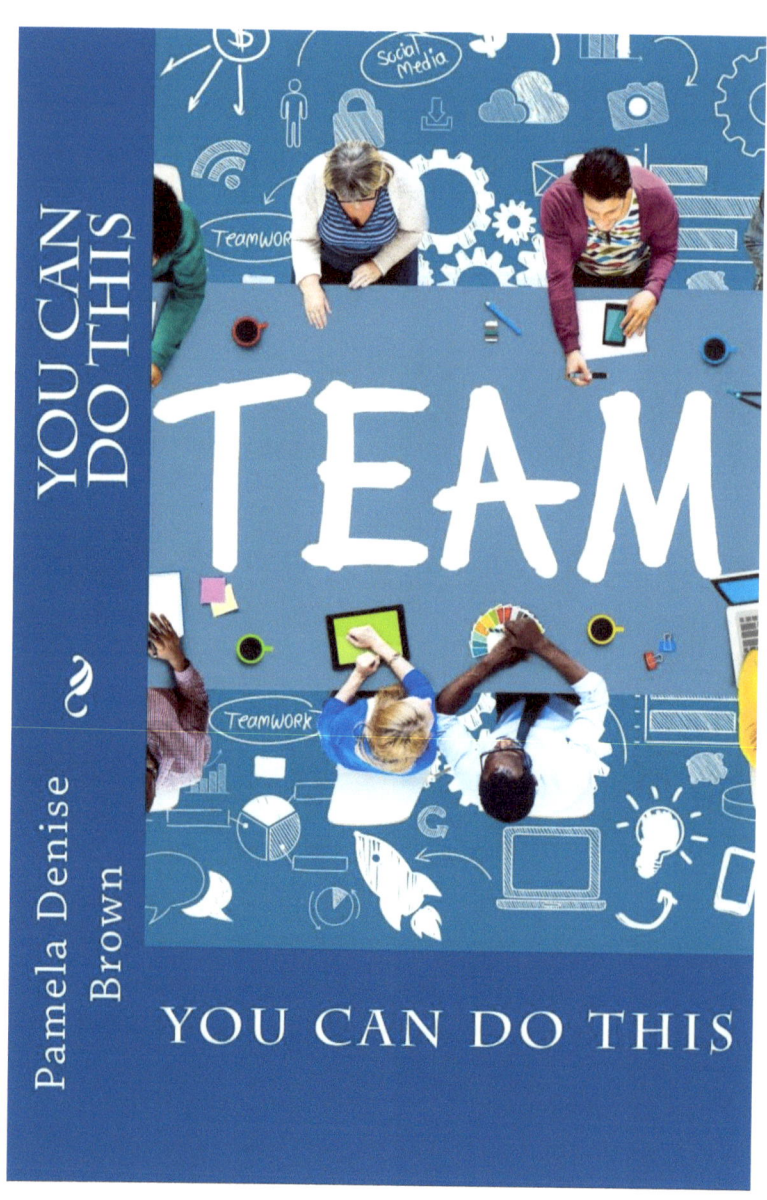

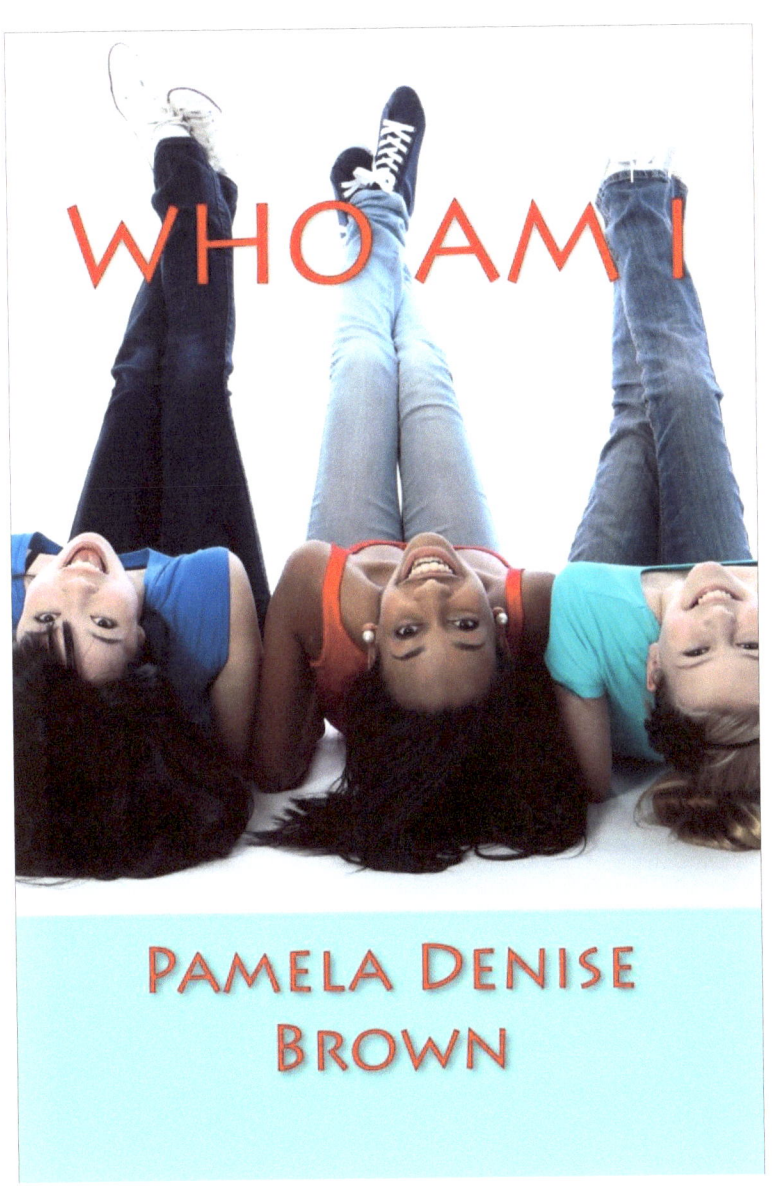

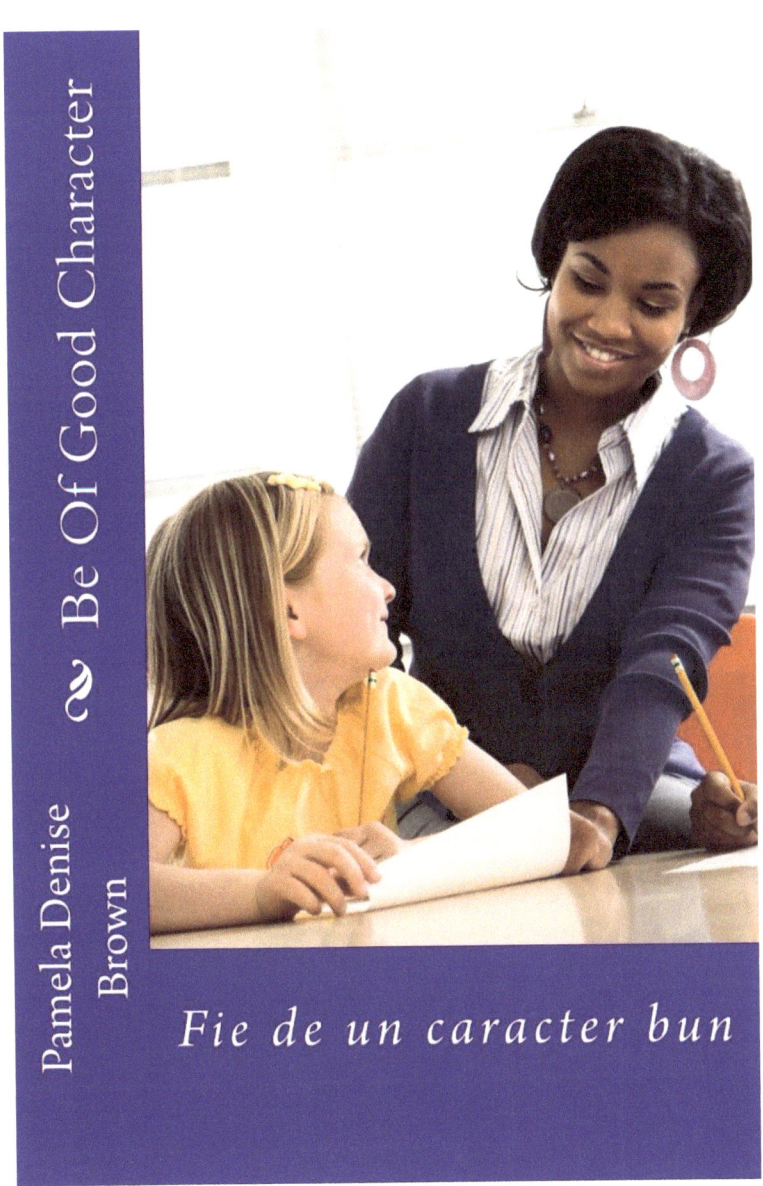

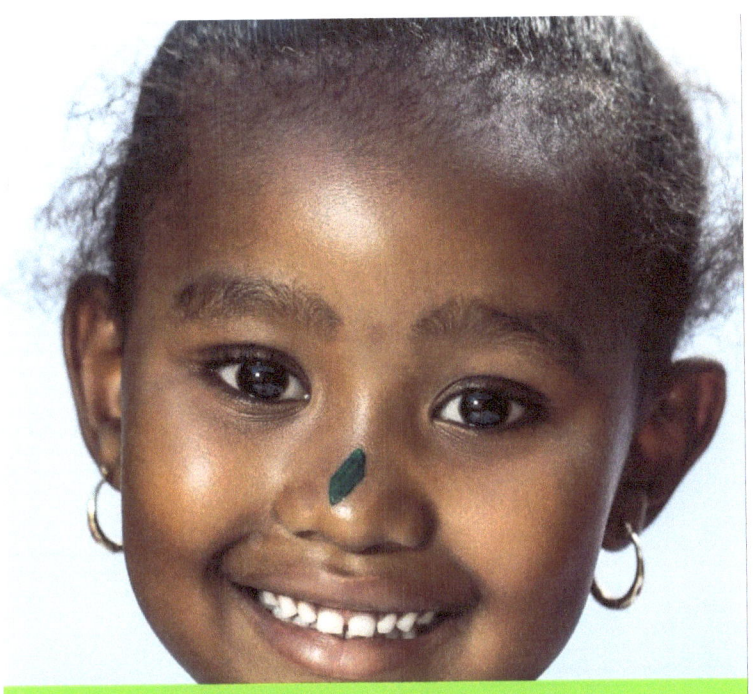

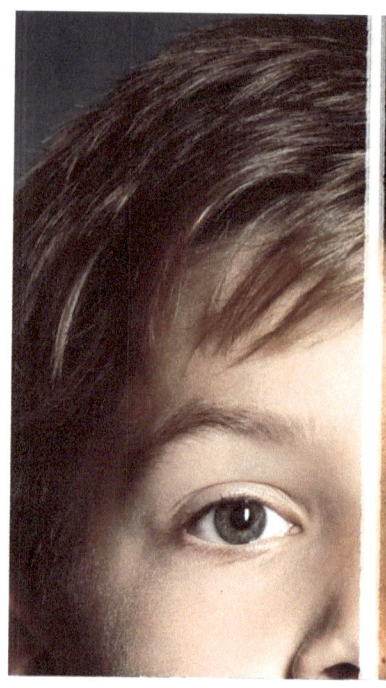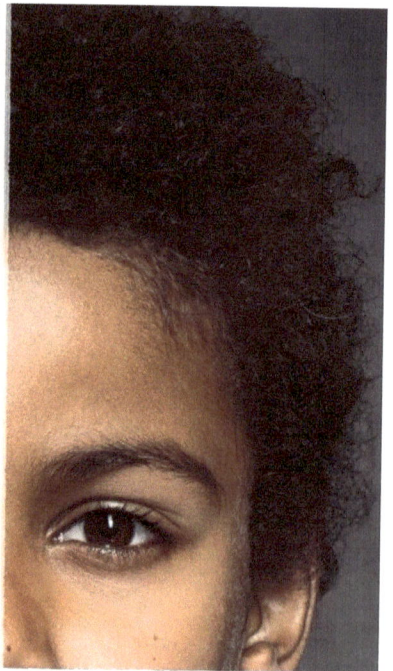

IT'S NOT BLACK OR WHITE IT'S ME

Pamela Denise Brown

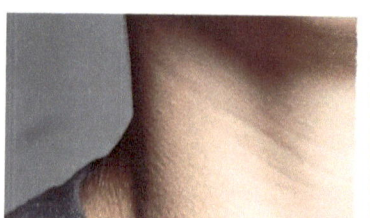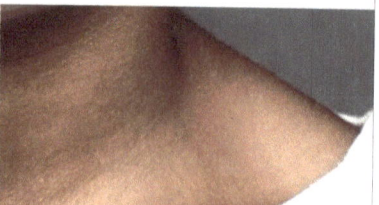

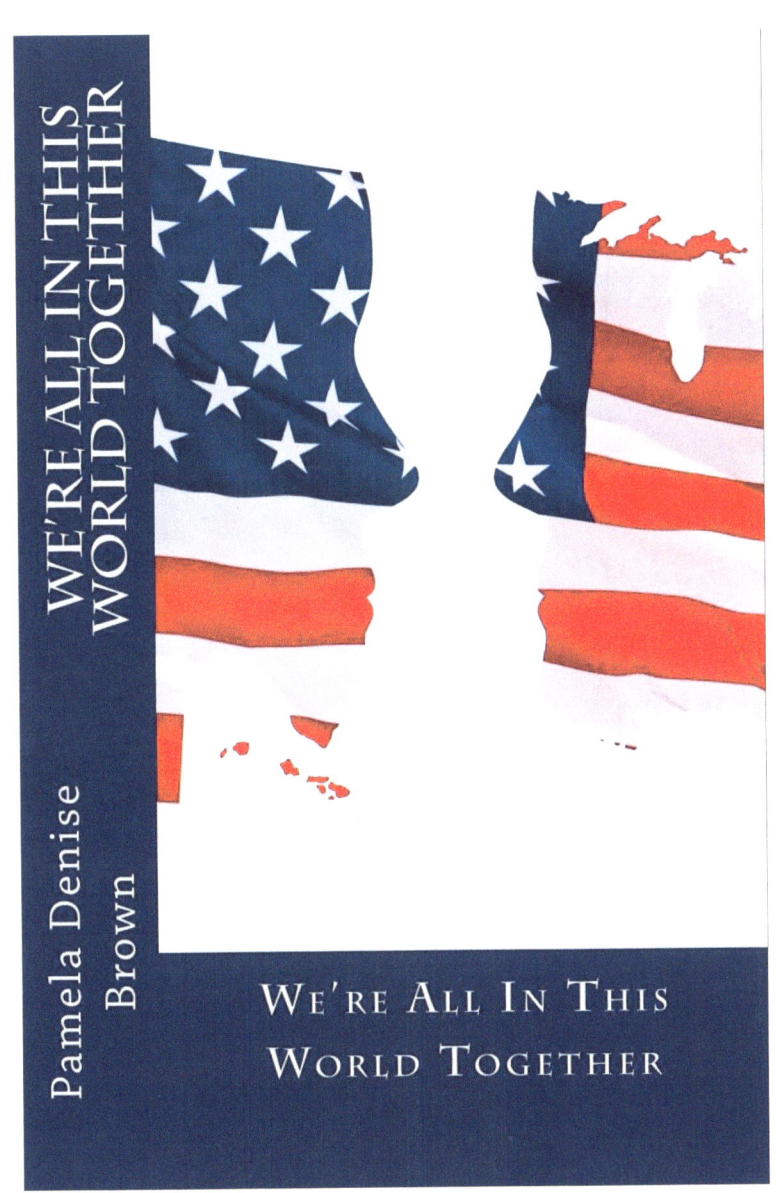

IT'S GOOD TO BE OPTIMISTIC

PAMELA DENISE BROWN

LEARN HOW TO BE GRATEFUL

Pamela Denise Brown

RECESS IS OVER

Pamela Denise Brown

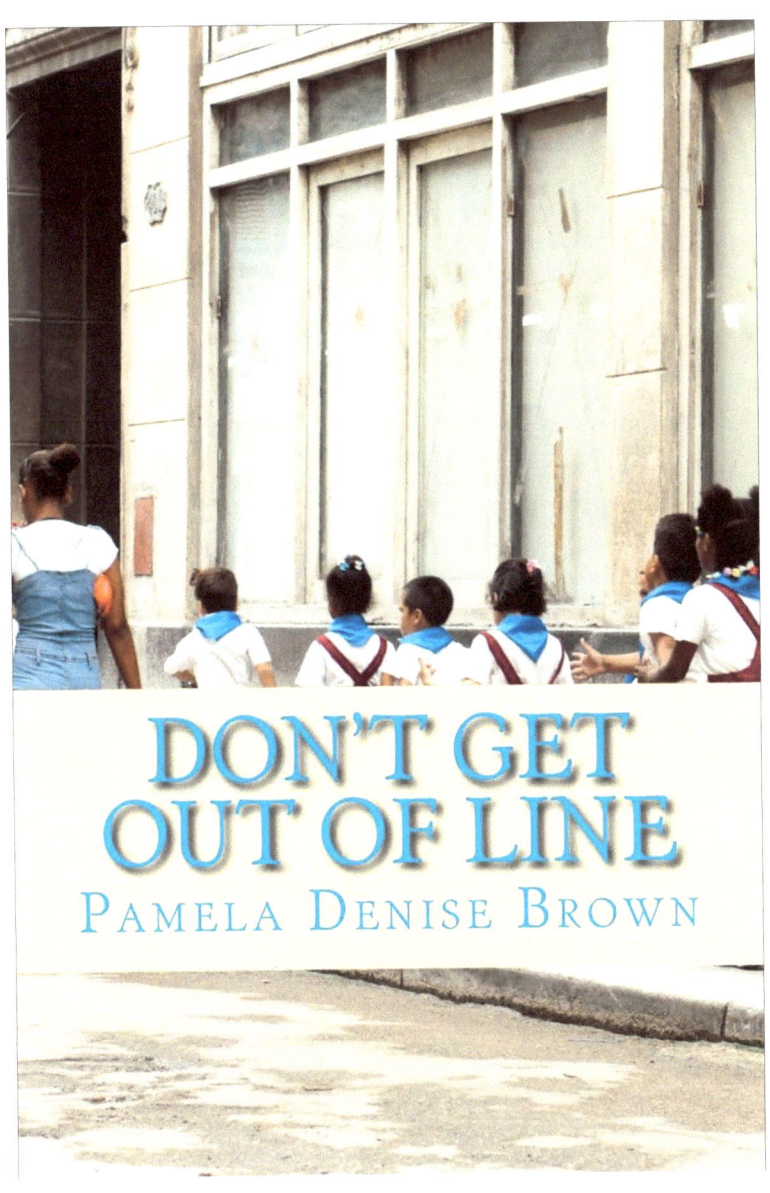

WHAT ARE YOU GOING TO DO IF IT'S TOO LATE

Pamela Denise Brown

Are You Paying Attention

Estas prestando atencion

PAMELA DENISE BROWN

WHY WOULD YOU WALK OUT OF CLASS

Pamela Denise Brown

Accept The Challenge

Acepta el desafio

Pamela Denise Brown

WHEN YOU RUN MAKE SURE YOU'RE NOT RUNNING FROM YOURSELF

Pamela Denise Brown

One Day The Rules Will Matter

Un dia Las Reglas importara

Pamela Denise Brown

What Does A Name Mean
Pamela Denise Brown

Don't Be A Dummy With A Smart Phone

No sea un maniqui con un telefono inteligente

Pamela Denise Brown

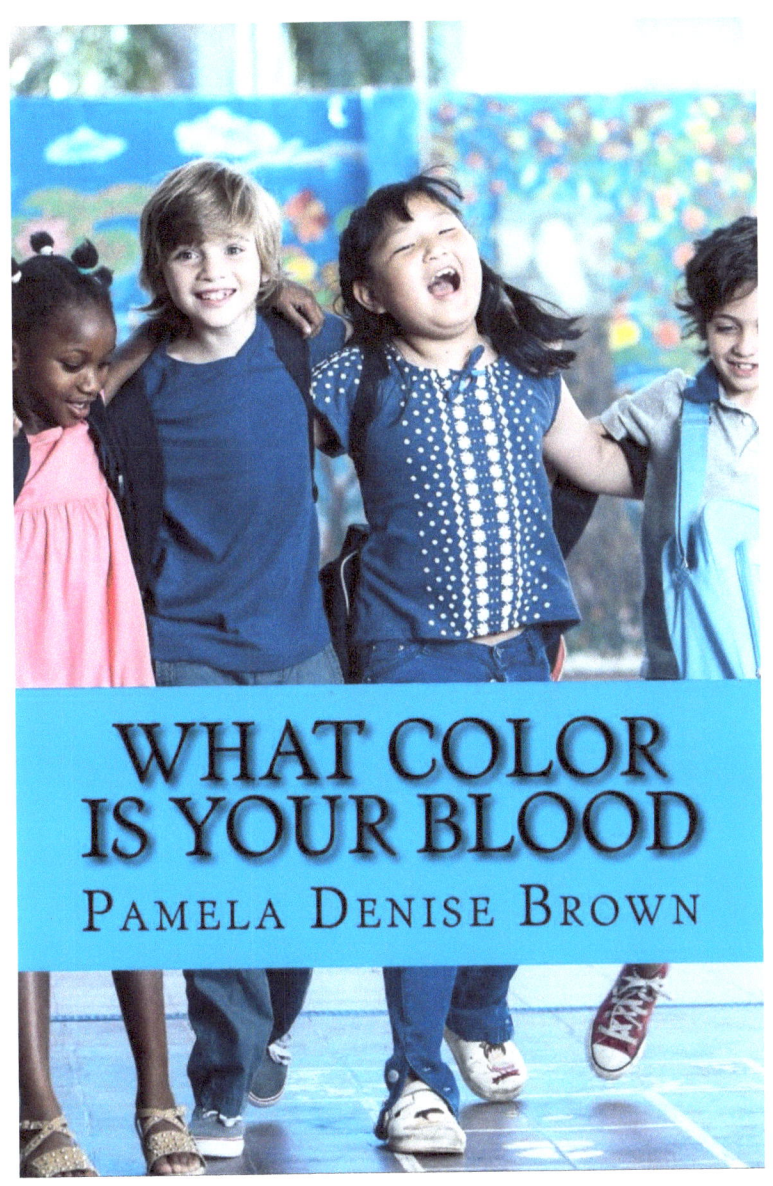

Disobedience Is Going To Cost You

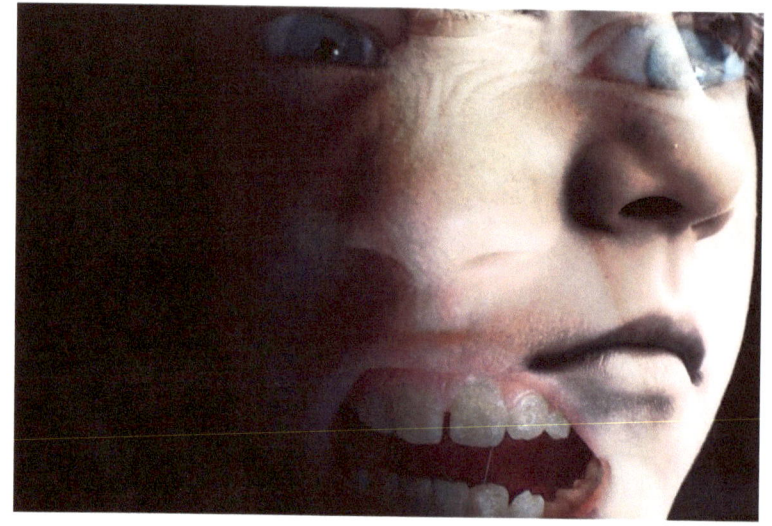

Desobediencia Se te va a costar

PAMELA DENISE BROWN

Thank You, Yes And Please The New Hello
Gracias Si y por favor, The New Hola

In The Morning I

Pamela Denise Brown

THE LAW IS FOR THE LAWLESS

Pamela Denise Brown

Good Morning I Hope Things Are Going Great Fantastic And Well For You

Pamela Denise Brown

What's A Flower

Pamela Denise Brown

Apa A Flower

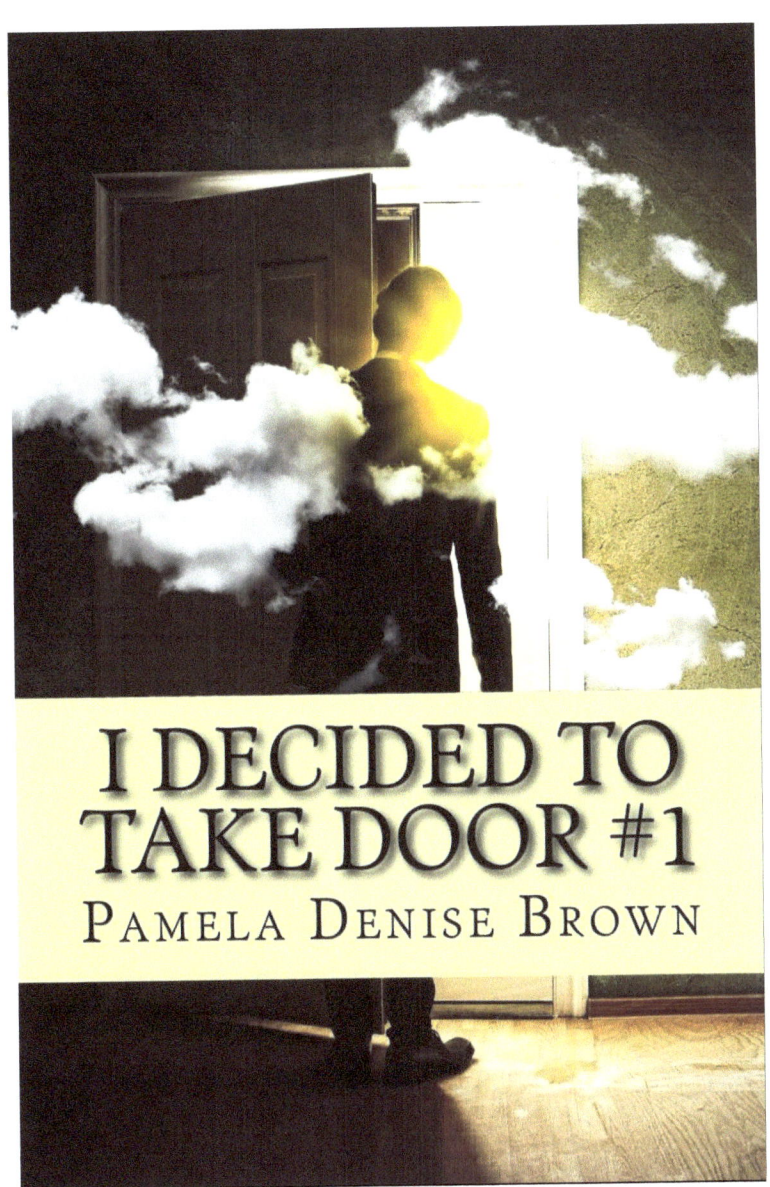

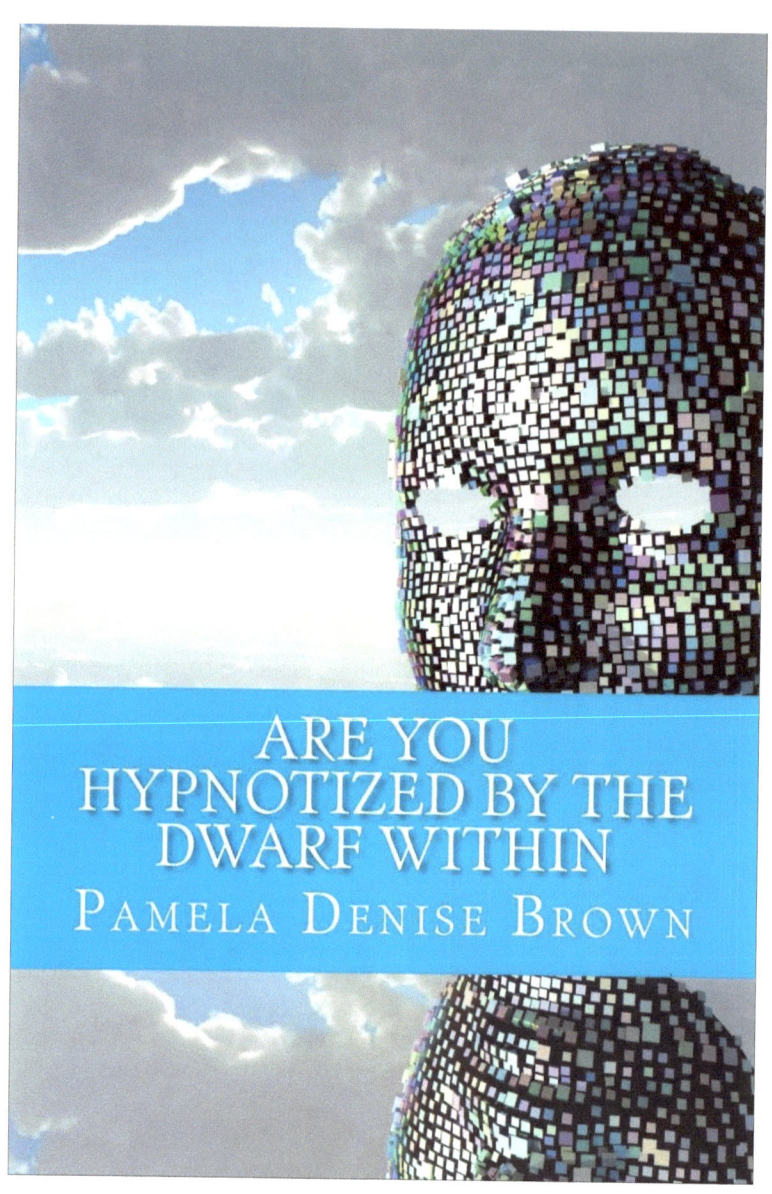

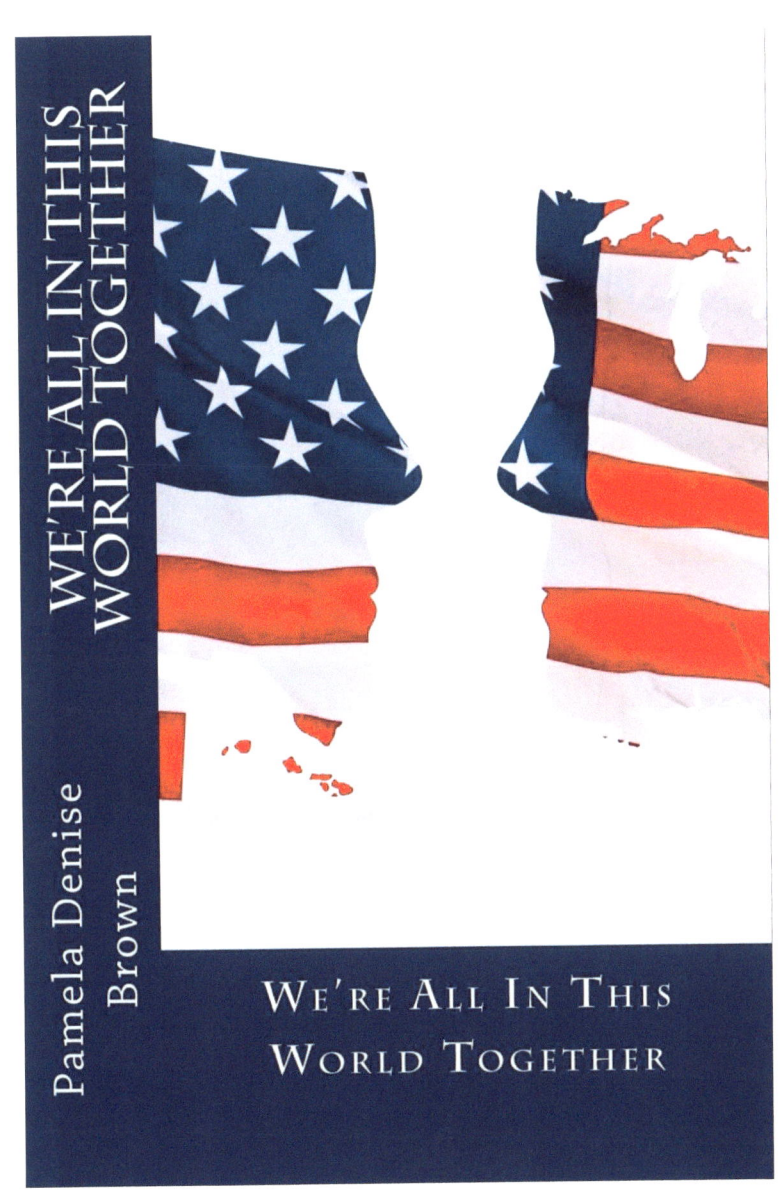

HOW DOES IT FEEL

Pamela Denise Brown

To

You, You, You

And Especially You,

You can

"Do Anything,

Be Anything, Become Anything"

MY TITLES speak volumes and even if you don't read the books,

The titles are speaking

TO YOU!!!!!

I typed all 100 books

On a laptop with 7 keys missing

Sometimes you have to inspire yourself...

All you need is YOU & GOD... you can do anything but FAIL....

But like everything in life,

You must take the FIRST STEP.........

Wishing You The Best I AM.

pamela denise brown

PEOPLE TO BE ACKNOWLEDGED WHO ACKNOWLEDGED ME

MY FIRST RUN.......

The Authors Show is a place where authors are given an opportunity to have their work acknowledged through web based radio and/or television interview. A place where you can be recognized for your literary accomplishments and sat on a platform where you're worked is viewed and appreciated. The Authors show was the first place I interviewed and for that I AM GRATEFUL... This is a thank you to the Authors Show and a SPECIAL Thank You to Linda Thompson, who interviewed me......

THANK YOU LINDA THOMPSON, Show Host

The Authors Show, www.TheAuthorsShow.com

The Authors Show, Nancy Villella, Production Assistant; TheAuthorsShow.com

The Authors Show, Danielle Hampson, Executive Producer; TheAuthorsShow.com

Thank You All For the Recognition....

www.ingramcontent.com/pod-product-compliance
Lightning Source LLC
Chambersburg PA
CBHW040302010526
44108CB00033B/10